This book
belongs to

Donated by:
Tiffany Patterson

This educational book was created in cooperation with Children's Television Workshop, producers of SESAME STREET. Children do not have to watch the television show to benefit from this book. Workshop revenues from this book will be used to help support CTW educational projects.

ON MY WAY WITH SESAME STREET

Volume 2

I Can Count

Featuring Jim Henson's Sesame Street Muppets
Children's Television Workshop/Funk & Wagnalls

Authors

Linda Hayward
Ray Sipherd
Jessie Smith
Norman Stiles
Lauren Collier Swindler

Illustrators

Tom Cooke
Tom Leigh
Kimberly A. McSparran
Nancy Stevenson
Joe Veno
Marsha Winborn

0-8343-0076-1

1 2 3 4 5 6 7 8 9 0

A Parents' Guide to I CAN COUNT

Understanding numbers is one of the most basic elements of a preschool education. Many children readily learn to recite the numbers from 1 to 10. It takes time, however, for them to understand that numbers are symbols for groups of objects: that counting is finding out "how many."

Once children can count the number of objects in a group, they can begin to recognize pre-math concepts such as "more/less" and "all/none." These concepts are the foundations for learning addition and subtraction.

In "Grover's Day at the Beach," children learn to recognize the numbers 1 to 12 and associate them with the concept of "how many." Along with Grover, children can count everything from old shoes to sea gulls to seashells.

"More/Less" and "All/None" are activities that demonstrate basic pre-math concepts. "Measure for Measure" introduces rulers, scales and other tools used to measure such things as height and weight.

In "Big Bird Brings Spring to Sesame Street," Big Bird introduces subtraction as he gives each of his friends a flower from his bouquet to brighten up a snowy day.

Once your children begin to feel comfortable with numbers, they are on their way to gaining the confidence they will need for beginning school.

The Editors
SESAME STREET BOOKS

Grover's Day at the Beach
A Counting Story

One day Grover Monster went to the beach with his friends. They
started to build a sand castle. Grover went down to the water's edge
with his pail.

"I will get some water for the moat," he said.

Grover spotted something blue and shiny in the wet sand.

"Oh, my goodness!" he said. "What have we here?"

He picked up an old bottle with a cork in the top. Then he noticed that there was something inside it.

"Hey, everybodee!" called Grover. "Look what I found!"

Grover's friends ran over to see.

"There's a message in the bottle, Grover!" said Betty Lou. "What does it say?"

Grover tugged and tugged on the cork. Finally it popped out of the bottle, and Grover pulled out a piece of paper.

"Today you will count to twelve," Grover read. "Oh, my goodness! All the way up to twelve! I wonder what to count first."

"You can start with the bottle," said Betty Lou.

"Right!" cried Grover. "One wonderful bottle!"

1

2

Two inflatable sea horses bobbed
in the water by the shore.

"Ernie and Bert must have parked their sea
horses here until they are ready to go paddling," said
Grover. "Meanwhile, I will count them!

"Two cute and adorable inflatable sea horses!

"Oh, dear," said Grover. "What shall I count now?"

"How about the waves, Grover?" asked the Count. "I love to count waves!"

"That is it, Count!" cried Grover. "I see three wonderful waves!"

3

4

5

It was a very busy day at the beach, and a very sunny one, too.

"I know!" said Grover. "I will count the colorful beach umbrellas. I see four. Four beach umbrellas."

Grover clumped on down the beach.

"Hey! I caught something!" Oscar yelled from the pier. "And what a great catch!"

"What is it, Oscar?" called Grover. Then he saw.

"Oh, well. I guess I can count five old shoes.

6

"Oh, dear," said Grover. "Whatever will I count now?"
"I have it, Grover!" said the Count. "Sailboats! I love to count sailboats."
Grover looked out to sea. He spied six sailboats with white sails.
"Six beautiful sailboats!" he counted happily.

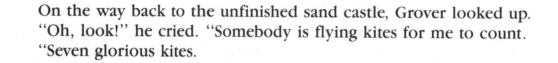

On the way back to the unfinished sand castle, Grover looked up. "Oh, look!" he cried. "Somebody is flying kites for me to count. "Seven glorious kites.

"Pant, pant!" said Grover when he got back to the sand castle. "Counting is very hard work! What will I count next?"

"How about sea gulls?" suggested the Count. "I love to count sea gulls."

High above their heads eight graceful sea gulls swooped and soared.

"Of course!" cried Grover. "Sea gulls. I will count them. Eight elegant sea gulls.

8

9

"We have important work to do besides counting," said Grover. "We must finish building the sand castle."

Cookie Monster happened by. He was eating a Popsicle.

"SLURP!" said Cookie. He ate up his Popsicle. Then he gave the stick to Grover, along with the other sticks in his fist.

"Oh, thank you, Cookie Monster!" said Grover. "I will make a Popsicle-stick fence for my sand castle.

"Nine Popsicle sticks."

Bert wanted to help, too.

"Here, Grover," he said. "These Figgy Fizz bottle caps are the finest from my collection. Would you like to use them? They would be keen on the sand castle!"

Grover and Bert carefully placed the bottle caps as windows all around the sand castle.

"Ten Figgy Fizz bottle caps!" Grover counted. "Terrific!"

10

11

"I found these shells on the beach, Grover," said Ernie. "Do you want them for the sand castle?"

"I am so lucky to have such thoughtful friends!" cried Grover. They put the seashells on the sand castle, one by one.

"Hmm..." said the Count. "I love to count seashells."

"Eleven super seashells!" said Grover.

"Oh, my goodness!" said Grover. "The message in the bottle said that I would count up to twelve today. I have only counted to eleven. What am I going to do? Maybe my friends will help me."

"Friends!" cried the Count. "I love to count friends."

"That is it!" said Grover. "I will count my friends. One, two, three, four, five, six, seven, eight, nine, ten, eleven friends...and me! That makes twelve wonderful friends. Terrific!"

The Count Counts

1 one castle

2 two bat cars

3 three capes

4 four towels

5 five family portraits

6 six bells

7 seven black cats

8 eight mirrors

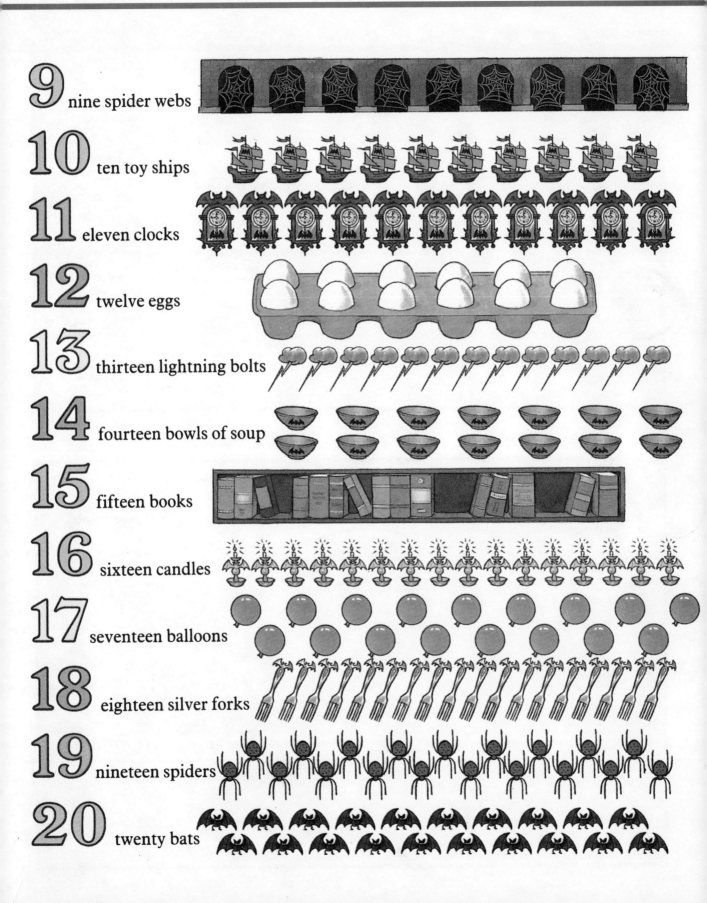

9 nine spider webs

10 ten toy ships

11 eleven clocks

12 twelve eggs

13 thirteen lightning bolts

14 fourteen bowls of soup

15 fifteen books

16 sixteen candles

17 seventeen balloons

18 eighteen silver forks

19 nineteen spiders

20 twenty bats

More

Cookie Monster has more cookies.

SOME   **MORE**

Who has more jelly sandwiches?

Less

Prairie Dawn has less lemonade.

MORE   **LESS**

Who has less salad?

The Count's Poem

Greetings! I am the Count. Do you know why they call me the Count? Because I LOVE to count things. And today I am counting some of my favorite things around the castle. Will you join me?

Counting can be lots of fun
When you start with number . . .

Now I have ONE candlestick to light our way.

Next, the number that is due
Is the lovely number . . .

Count with the Count

How many lightning bolts do you see?
Point to the correct number on the banner.

How many pianos do you see?   How many portraits?

How many kittens?   How many bats?

The Three Monsters

Once upon a time there were three
monsters—a Great Big Monster,
a Middle-Sized Monster,
and a Wee Little Monster.

One day they went to the beach. Each monster
took a pail and shovel. The Great Big Monster took
a great big pail and shovel. The Middle-Sized
Monster took a middle-sized pail and shovel. And
the Wee Little Monster took a wee little pail and
shovel.

Which pail and shovel belong to each monster?

When they arrived at the beach, each monster built a sand castle. The Great Big Monster built a great big sand castle. The Middle-Sized Monster built a middle-sized sand castle. And the Wee Little Monster built a wee little sand castle.

Which sand castle was built by each monster?

Then each monster sat down in a beach chair. The Great Big Monster sat down in a great big beach chair. The Middle-Sized Monster sat down in a middle-sized beach chair. And the Wee Little Monster sat down in a wee little beach chair.

Which beach chair belongs to each monster?

Then the three monsters went for a swim. While they were gone, Betty Lou came to deliver sandwiches from the sandwich store.

"Oh, dear," she said. "I have a great big salami sandwich and a middle-sized bologna sandwich and a wee little pastrami sandwich, and I don't know whom to deliver them to."

Just then the three monsters came out of the water.

Do *you* know what sandwich belongs to which monster?

Big Bird Brings Spring to Sesame Street

BIG BIRD looked down Sesame Street. Everything was covered with a thick layer of white snow. Big Bird sighed. It had been a long winter. He was tired of looking at plain white snow.

So Big Bird walked down to Mr. MacIntosh's store and bought six of his favorite flowers.

"I feel better already," thought Big Bird as he walked back toward Sesame Street with his bouquet of six beautiful flowers.

On the way to his nest, Big Bird stopped at the Count's castle.

"Ah, Big Bird, what beautiful flowers!" cried the Count. "Let me count them. One beautiful flower, two beautiful flowers, three, four, five, six beautiful flowers.

"Big Bird, I love counting your beautiful flowers."

"Gee, I didn't buy the flowers to count them," said Big Bird. "I bought them to remind me of spring. Would you like to keep this pretty pink daisy? You can count all of its petals."

"Wonderful!" cried the Count. "One pretty petal, two pretty petals..."

Big Bird walked down Sesame Street, carrying his five flowers. He stopped to watch Maria shovel snow from the sidewalk in front of the Fix-it Shop.

Oops! Maria fell in the snow.

"Oh, Maria, are you hurt?" asked Big Bird as he helped her stand up.

"No, Big Bird, I'm not hurt. But I am tired of winter and snow," she said.

"Here, Maria," said Big Bird. "You may have one of my flowers. It will help you feel happy again."

"Thank you, Big Bird," said Maria, taking the orange tiger lily.

Big Bird walked on down Sesame Street with the four flowers he had left. He found Grover sitting sadly on the steps.

"Oh, my goodness," said Grover unhappily. "Furry old Grover is very blue."

"Maybe this blue pansy will make you feel better," said Big Bird, and he gave it to Grover.

Big Bird looked down at his three flowers. "Uh-oh," said Big Bird, holding up the purple iris. "This flower's stem is broken."

"I love things that are broken!" said Oscar-the-Grouch, leaning out of his can.

"Gee, Oscar, take my purple iris."

"Thanks, Bird," said Oscar. "Grouches like flowers that are bent and broken. Heh, heh, heh." He grabbed the purple iris and slammed down the lid of the trash can.

Big Bird clutched his last two flowers. Then he saw Ernie.
"Where are you going?" asked Big Bird.
"I'm going to see Betty Lou. She's sick in bed with the flu," said Ernie.

"I wish I had something to take her to cheer her up...."
"Oh," said Big Bird, "do you think she would like a yellow daffodil?"
"Oh, yes! Thank you, Big Bird."

Big Bird went into Hooper's Store to get warm. Bert was sadly sipping his Figgy Fizz.
"What's wrong, Bert?" asked Big Bird.
"I've lost my favorite paper clip in a snowdrift," wailed Bert.
"Now I'll have to wait until the snow melts to find it."

"Your paper clip will still be there in the spring," said Big Bird.

Bert looked at Big Bird's single rose.

"What are you going to do with that beautiful rose?" he asked.

"Uh, er . . . I'm going to give it to you, Bert." Big Bird gave Bert his last flower and left.

Empty-handed, Big Bird walked back up Sesame Street. He had given away all six of his flowers. "Oh, well," he thought. "Soon it will be spring."

When he got to the lamppost, Big Bird turned around.

Sesame Street looked different! The plain, white, snow-covered street was splashed with bright colors. The flowers Big Bird had given to his friends were blooming. Big Bird had brought spring to Sesame Street.

The Magic Trick

The Amazing Mumford waved his wand.

Out of his hat came 1 RABBIT.

The Amazing Mumford waved his wand again.

Out of his hat came another rabbit. How many rabbits are there now? 1 RABBIT and 1 MORE RABBIT make 2 RABBITS.

The Amazing Mumford waved his wand *again*.

Out of his hat came *another* rabbit. How many rabbits are there now? 2 RABBITS and 1 MORE RABBIT make 3 RABBITS.

The Amazing Mumford waved his wand once more.

Out of his hat came one more rabbit. How many rabbits are there now? 3 RABBITS and 1 MORE RABBIT make 4 RABBITS.

Measure for Measure

Bert wants to measure his birdhouse. What does he need?

Cookie wants to measure flour to make some cookies. What does he need?

The doctor wants to measure Betty Lou's weight. What does she need?

Grover's mommy wants to measure Grover's height. What does she need?

All

This Twiddlebug has all the flower petals.

NONE

ALL

Who has all the cookies?

None

This cubby has none of the toys.

ALL

NONE

Which basket has none of the strawberries?

One, two, three, four, five, six, seven, eight...**8** Susannas with banjos on their knees!

One, two, three, four, five, six, seven, eight, nine...**9** horses!

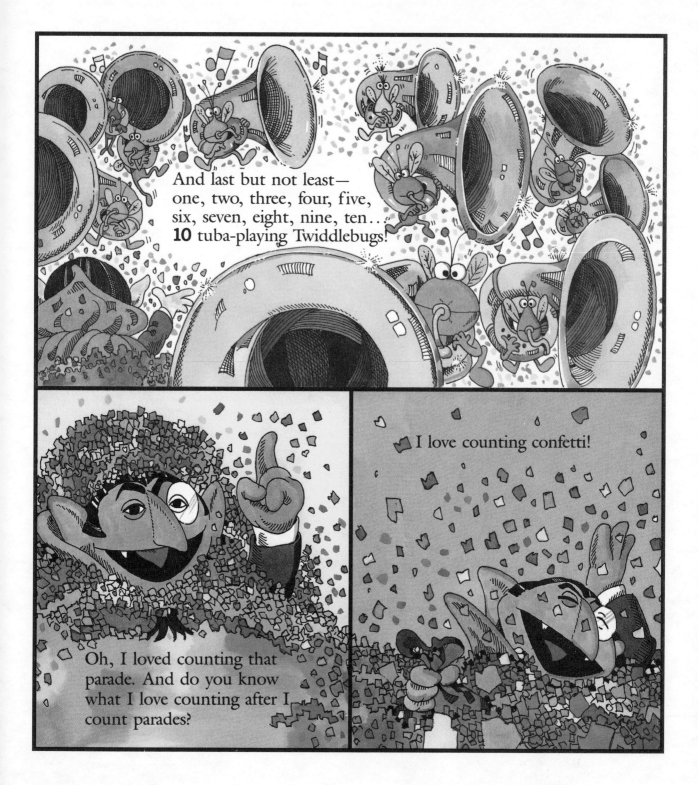